Dog B

Facts for Fun!

Book C-D

By Wyatt Michaels

Copyright 2012

Image courtesy of History Rewound

Some of these dogs were imported to the United States by George Washington.

   A. Dalmatian
   B. Coonhound
   C. Doberman Pinscher

Image courtesy of Scraig

The answer is B. Coonhound

President Washington had four Black and Tan Coonhounds like the one pictured.

Image courtesy of Matthew Kenwrick

This breed was the mascot for the 1972 summer Olympics in Munich, Germany.

A. Doberman Pinscher
B. Dalmatian
C. Dachshund

Image courtesy of Howard O. Young

The answer is C. Dachshund

Because dachshunds are associated with Germany, Waldi (a dachshund) was chosen as the first official mascot of the Olympics in Germany.

Image courtesy of wadem

What is not a specific breed, but is a type of herding dog?

A. Coonhound
B. Collie
C. Dalmatian

Image courtesy of ThreeDee912

The answer is B. Collie

Collies originated in northern England and Scotland. Types of collies include Rough Collie, Smooth Collie and Shetland Sheepdogs or Shelties.

Image courtesy of David Shankbone

Martha Stewart had one of these named Genghis Khan.

A. Chow Chow
B. Doberman Pinscher
C. Cockapoo

Image courtesy of Hey Paul

The answer is A. Chow Chow

Drew Barrymore, Selena Gomez, and
Matthew McConaughey had Chow-
Labrador mixes.

Image courtesy of RMTip21

A dog of this breed named Smokey is the mascot of University of Tennessee.

A. Collie
B. Dalmatian
C. Coonhound

Image courtesy of public domain

The answer is C. Coonhound

Smokey is a Bluetick Coonhound like the one in the picture.

Image courtesy of tourist on earth

This breed played Luca in the 2004 movie, "Garfield: the Movie".

A. Doberman Pinscher

B. Chihuahua

C. Dalmatian

Image courtesy of andrewk100

The answer is A. Doberman Pinscher

Also, in the Disney movie, "Oliver & Company", Roscoe and DeSoto are Dobermans.

Image courtesy of pioneerpeststl

This breed is associated with Budweiser's horse-drawn carriage.

A. Collie

B. Coonhound

C. Dalmatian

Image courtesy of pulkitsinha

The answer is C. Dalmatian

It is said that Dalmatians used to guard the wagons while the driver made deliveries for breweries.

Image courtesy of foto-junky once in a while
photography

What is the smallest dog breed?

A. Dachshund
B. Chihuahua
C. Cockapoo

Image courtesy of Tyke

The answer is B. Chihuahua

At least they are the smallest breed recognized by some kennel clubs. Boo Boo, a long-haired Chihuahua is said to be the smallest dog at 4 inches tall and weighing 2 pounds.

Which breed is a cross between an American or English Cocker Spaniel and a poodle?

A. Cockapoo

B. Chihuahua

C. Dachshund

Image courtesy of ALMM

The answer is A. Cockapoo

They are popular because of the outgoing, loving personality of the Cocker Spaniel combined with the low-shedding, low-dander qualities of the Poodle. Cuteness has to be a factor, too!

Image courtesy of Les Stockton

President Calvin Coolidge owned a
black one of these named "Timmy".

A. Chow Chow
B. Coonhound
C. Dalmatian

Image courtesy of Remigiusz Jozefowicz

The answer is A. Chow Chow

Coolidge was President in the 1920's when Chow Chows were popular among the rich and famous.

Image courtesy of Neal Young

The name of this breed means "badger dog".

A. Chihuahua
B. Dachshund
C. Doberman Pinscher

Image courtesy of Blues La Nanasim

The answer is B. Dachshund

They were bred to scent, chase, and flush out badgers and other burrowing animals such as prairie dogs.

Image courtesy of r-z

Which breed is featured in the book, Where the Red Fern Grows?

A. Collie
B. Doberman Pinscher
C. Coonhound

Image courtesy of apswartz

The answer is C. Coonhound

The type of Coonhound in that book is called a Redbone Coonhound just like the pup in the picture.

Image courtesy of Steven Wilke

Reveille, The official mascot of Texas A & M is one of these.

A. Collie

B. Dalmatian

C. Doberman Pinscher

Image courtesy of Varin Tsai

The answer is A. Collie

Another famous collie, Silverton Bobbie, traveled 2,800 miles to return home to Silverton, OR from Indiana.

Image courtesy of Loren Javier

What breed is Old Towser in 101
Dalmatians?

A. Cockapoo
B. Coonhound
C. Dachshund

Image courtesy of Shames Privacy

The answer is B. Coonhound

Technically, Old Towser was a Bloodhound which is in the same "family" as a Coonhound.

Image courtesy of Wiertz Sebastien

This breed was the war dog of the
Marine Corps during World War II.

   A. Doberman Pinscher
   B. Chow Chow
   C. Dachshund

Image courtesy of public domain

The answer is A. Doberman Pinscher

A Doberman named Kurt saved the lives of 250 Marines in WWII. Kurt's name along with 24 other Dobermans are inscribed on the WWII War Dog Memorial.

Image courtesy of Helga Weber

Which breed gots its name from the area it came from?

    A. Chow Chow

    B. Dachshund

    C. Chihuahua

Image courtesy of Toronja Azul

The answer is C. Chihuahua

Chihuahuas come from the state of Chihuahua in Mexico.

Image courtesy of tncountryfan

This breed is considered a firehouse mascot from the days of nipping horses' heels to get them to run faster.

A. Dalmatian

B. Collie

C. Doberman Pinscher

Image courtesy of tinyfroglet

The answer is A. Dalmatian

Pi Kappa Alpha, known as the firefighter's fraternity, also has the Dalmatian for their mascot.

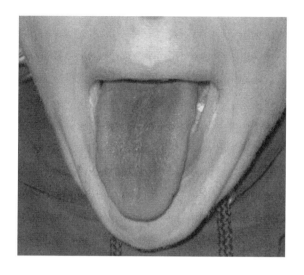

Image courtesy of estro

Which breed is distinguished by its blue/black/purple tongue?

A. Dalmatian

B. Coonhound

C. Chow Chow

Image courtesy of golbenge

The answer is C. Chow Chow

Sometimes the bluish color extends to their lips.

Image courtesy of gothopotam

What breed was Lassie in the classic TV series called Lassie?

A. Collie
B. Dachshund
C. Coonhound

Image courtesy of public domain

The answer is A. Collie

Lassie was a Rough Collie who went on to star in many MGM movies.

Image courtesy of wackybadger

This breed is capable of following the scent of animals on the ground and up trees.

  A. Coonhound
  B. Chow Chow
  C. Doberman Pinscher

Image courtesy of Jayaebee

The answer is A. Coonhound

They are used to track and tree raccoons, bobcats, cougars, and bears. They can also catch opossums, skunks, and squirrels.

Image courtesy of the Italian voice

This is the only breed that can hunt above and below ground.

A. Coonhound
B. Dachshund
C. Cockapoo

Image courtesy of public domain

The answer is B. Dachshund

They are used to hunt badgers, rabbits, foxes, and even bigger animals such as wild boar and locate wounded deer.

Image courtesy of lisaclarke

Which breed likes to burrow in pillows, clothes hampers, and blankets?

A. Cockapoo
B. Dachshund
C. Chihuahua

Image courtesy of whatjeanlikes

The answer is C. Chihuahua

They can often be found deep in some dark place that they believe is safe.

Image courtesy of jonlclark

El Diablo in the 2008 movie "Beverly Hills Chihuahua" was one of these.

A. Doberman Pinscher
B. Dalmatian
C. Collie

Image courtesy of pato Garza

The answer is A. Doberman Pinscher

Also, Alpha in the 2009 film "Up" is a Doberman.

Image courtesy of Glyn Lowe Photoworks

President Grover Cleveland had one of these in the White House.

A. Chow Chow
B. Dachshund
C. Collie

Image courtesy of public domain

The answer is B. Dachshund

The original Wizard of Oz initially had a dachshund as Dorothy's pet. Toto was a more politically correct breed at the time (post WWII), so Otto the dachshund was replaced.

Image courtesy of karola riegler photography

Pongo, Mrs. Pongo, Patch, Lucky, Perdita, and Prince are famous, but fictional dogs of this breed.

A. Cockapoo
B. Dalmatian
C. Chihuahua

Image courtesy of Mago tecnologico

The answer is B. Dalmatian

They are just a few of the 101
Dalmatians.

Image courtesy of Daisyree Bakker

This breed can run for miles and is good for hunting bear, deer, and cougars.

    A. Coonhound
    B. Doberman Pinscher
    C. Collie

Image courtesy of Natalie Maynor

The answer is A. Coonhound

These dogs are known for their courage, as well as ability to cover ground quickly.

Image courtesy of ChicagoGeek

Which breed was featured in the movies "The Shaggy Dog" in 2006, and "Hotel for Dogs" in 2009?

A. Chihuahua
B. Dachshund
C. Collie

Image courtesy of wuestenigel

The answer is C. Collie

Shep is a Border Collie in "Hotel for Dogs". Shaggy is a Bearded Collie that was featured in "The Shaggy Dog".

Image courtesy of puuikibeach

What breed originated in China and its name is translated "puffy-lion dog"?

A. Chihuahua
B. Chow Chow
C. Doberman Pinscher

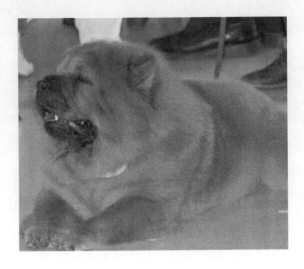

Image courtesy of Ger Dekker

The answer is B. Chow Chow

The thick fur in its neck area gives the breed a look somewhat like the mane of a lion.

Congratulations! You can now impress your family and friends with what you know about dog breeds that start with "c" or "d".

Look for more quiz books by Wyatt Michaels about other dog breeds, baseball, letter sounds, careers, football, horses, presidents, states, and more.

Printed in Great Britain
by Amazon.co.uk, Ltd.,
Marston Gate.